Pebble® Plus

A Visit to
The Fire Station

Revised Edition

T0061185

4D
Download the Capstone 4D app for additional content.

4D See page 2 for directions.

by Blake A. Hoena

CAPSTONE PRESS
a capstone imprint

Download the Capstone 4D app!

- Ask an adult to search in the Apple App Store or Google Play for "Capstone 4D".
- Click Install (Android) or Get, then Install (Apple).
- Open the app.
- Scan any of the following spreads with this icon:

When you scan a spread, you'll find fun extra stuff to go with this book!
You can also find these things on the web at www.capstone4D.com
using the password: **fire.08291**

Pebble Plus is published by Capstone Press,
1710 Roe Crest Drive, North Mankato, Minnesota 56003
www.mycapstone.com

Library of Congress Cataloging-in-Publication Data
is available on the Library of Congress website.

ISBN 978-1-5435-0829-1 (library binding)
ISBN 978-1-5435-0841-3 (paperback)
ISBN 978-1-5435-0869-7 (ebook pdf)

Editorial Credits
Sarah Bennett, designer; Tracy Cummins, media researcher;
Laura Manthe, production specialist

Photo Credits
Capstone Press: Gary Sundermeyer, 3, 5, 7, 9, 11, 13, 15, 17, 19,
21; Shutterstock: amirage, Design Element, Monkey Business
Images, Cover Left, planet5D LL, Cover Background

Note to Parents and Teachers

The A Visit to set supports national social studies standards
related to the production, distribution, and consumption of
goods and services. This book describes and illustrates a fire
station. The images support early readers in understanding the
text. The repetition of words and phrases helps early readers
learn new words. This book also introduces early readers to
subject-specific vocabulary words, which are defined in the
Glossary section. Early readers may need assistance to read
some words and to use the Table of Contents, Glossary, Read
More, Internet Sites, Critical Thinking Questions, and Index
sections of the book.

Table of Contents

The Fire Station

A fire station is a fun

place to visit.

NEW ULM
FIRE DEPT. 5

Trucks and Gear

Fire engines have flashing lights and loud horns.

Fire engines and other trucks park in the bay.

Some fire trucks carry ladders.
Ladders can reach the tops of
tall buildings.

Firefighters wear coats, helmets, and boots.
The heavy gear keeps them safe.

Around the Fire Station

Dispatchers tell firefighters how
to get to a fire quickly.
Dispatchers listen to radios,
look at maps, and answer calls.

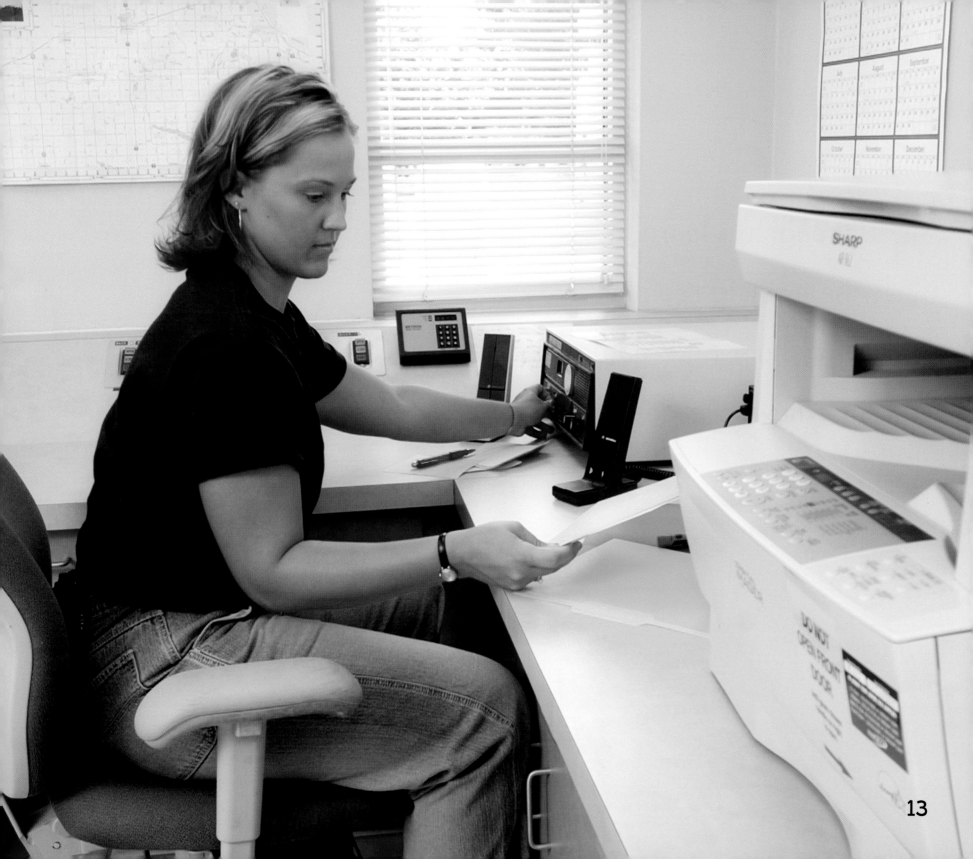

Firefighters learn in
the training room.
They hear and see how to
use new safety equipment.

Firefighters exercise in
the dorm during the day.
They rest in beds at night.

Firefighters cook meals
in the kitchen.
They eat together
during breaks.

Working Together

People at the fire station

work together to keep

their community safe.

Glossary

bay—the area in a fire station where trucks and other firefighting equipment is kept; the bay is on the ground floor so that trucks can drive onto the street

dorm—a room or a building with beds; another word for dorm is dormitory

fire engine—a large truck that carries firefighting equipment to a fire; firefighters also ride on fire engines

gear—a set of clothing or equipment; firefighters wear heavy coats, pants, and boots called bunker gear

truck—a vehicle; fire stations use many different kinds of trucks; pumper trucks carry and pump water; ladder trucks carry tall ladders to fires

Read More

Martin, Isabel. *A Fire Station Field Trip.* Let's Take a Field Trip. North Mankato, Minn.: Capstone, 2015.

Murray, Julie. *The Fire Station.* My Community: Places. Minneapolis: Abdo Kids, 2017.

Siemens, Jared. *Firefighter.* People in My Neighborhood. New York: Smartbook Media Inc., 2018.

Internet Sites

Use FactHound to find Internet sites related to this book.

Visit *www.facthound.com*

Just type **9781543508291** and go.

 **Super-cool stuff!** Check out projects, games and lots more at **www.capstonekids.com**

Critical Thinking Questions

1. Describe what firefighters wear to stay safe.

2. What does a dispatcher do?

3. Would you want to work at a fire station? Why or why not?

Index